Withdrawn

LIGHTNING

Sheets, Streaks,
Beads, and Balls

LIGHTNING

by Suzanne Harper

A First Book

FRANKLIN WATTS

A DIVISION OF GROLIER PUBLISHING
New York ■ London ■ Hong Kong ■ Sydney
Danbury, Connecticut

For every writing teacher who taught me the difference between lightning and a lightning bug

Photographs ©: Art Resource: 11 (Erich Lessing); Comstock: cover; Corbis-Bettmann: 17; John J. Morgan, Jr.: 29; Kent Wood: 30, 51, 54; North Wind Picture Archives: 32; Photo Researchers: 45 (John Deeks), 43 (John R. Foster), 36 (Phillip Hayson), 41 (Keith Kent), 2 (John Mead/SPL), 14 (James Robinson), 8, 48 (Kent Wood); Reuters/Corbis-Bettmann: 26, 35.

Illustrations by Lloyd Birmingham

Library of Congress Cataloging-in-Publication Data

Harper, Suzanne.
Lightning: sheets, streaks, beads, and balls / by Suzanne Harper
p. cm. — (A First book)
Includes bibliographical references and index.
Summary: Discusses ancient legends about lightning as well as what scientists have learned about this phenomenon in recent years and includes information about thundercloud and lightning formation, types of lightning, and safety tips.
ISBN 0-531-20290-9
1. Lightning—Juvenile literature. [1. Lightning.] I. Title. II. Series.
QC966.5.H37 1997
551.5'632—dc20

96-33299
CIP
AC

CONTENTS

INTRODUCTION

rash! Ka-boom! A brilliant flash of light turns night into day as a lightning bolt strikes the ground and thunder echoes through the air. Lightning strikes the earth 50 to 100 times every single second. That adds up to 8 million or 9 million strikes every day. Each year, about 40 million lightning bolts hit the ground in the United States.

Right now, roughly 2,000 thunderstorms are raging on our planet. A typical thunderstorm contains about the same amount of energy as ten atomic bombs. Although most lightning bolts discharge

Lightning strikes the Earth 8 or 9 million times every day—or 50 to 100 times every second.

between 10 million and 30 million volts of energy, some carry as much as 100 million volts. That is millions of times the power provided by the huge electric generators in a power plant, although it lasts for only a brief time.

Lightning can destroy trees or buildings, start forest fires, and kill animals and people. It's an awesome phenomenon that has fascinated humans for centuries.

Ancient Beliefs

In ancient times, people didn't know what caused lightning, so they made up stories to explain it. Many cultures believed in more than one god, and the sky god—the one in charge of thunder and lightning—was often the most powerful of all.

For example, more than 5,000 years ago, people in Babylon believed that the god Adad carried a boomerang in one hand to cause thunder and a spear in the other hand to cause lightning. Ancient Persians believed in a god called Apam Napat who took the form of a thundercloud and wore lightning for clothes.

The ancient Greeks believed that lightning belonged to Zeus, the king of gods.

Zeus was the king of the gods, according to the ancient Greeks. Lightning belonged to Zeus, so any spot that was struck by lightning was considered sacred. Three one-eyed giants, called Cyclopes, made thunderbolts for Zeus to throw at earth.

The ancient Romans called the king of their gods Jupiter. They believed that the oak tree, which was a symbol of Jupiter, was hit by lightning more often than other trees. They also thought that lightning never hit bay laurel trees. For this reason, the Roman emperor Tiberius wore laurel whenever a thunderstorm threatened. After a victory in battle, Roman generals wore laurel wreaths to protect themselves from the jealous anger of the thunder god.

On the other side of the world, the Chinese goddess of lightning was believed to travel with the thunder god. She carried mirrors in each hand to flash a bright light on the thunder god's path so he could see where to send his thunderbolts.

According to some historians, Thursday was named after Thor, the Norse god of thunder and lightning. The Norsemen believed that thunder was the sound made by the wheels of Thor's chariot as he rode around the heavens, and that lightning occurred whenever Thor threw his red-hot hammer.

In southwestern Nigeria, Yoruba priests held ceremonies in which they asked the thunder-and-lightning god Sango to ward off violent storms. Some African tribes believed that lightning was caused by a thunderbird, which laid eggs with magical healing powers.

Native American tribes had different myths about what caused thunder and lightning. The eastern tribes believed in a flock of god-birds called the Thunderers. Thunder was the sound of their wings, and lightning was created when they struck their beaks against trees in search of food. Western tribes believed that the god of thunder was one great bird—called the Thunderbird—and that lightning was a flash from its eye. Southwestern tribes thought lightning was a snake that traveled from the heavens to the earth.

During the Middle Ages, people in northern Europe thought that lightning was created by witches, so they made up spells to protect themselves. They believed that burning a Yule log on Christmas Eve or a bonfire on Midsummer's Eve would protect their homes for a year. They also believed that anyone who carried splinters from a lightning-struck tree would not be struck by lightning.

In France, people searched through fields after storms for "thunderstones," small oblong pieces of rock. The French believed that these rocks, which may have actually been tools or objects made by people dur-

ing the *Stone Age*, were the spearheads of lightning bolts that had hit the ground. Peasants carried the stones in their pockets to ward off lightning. When they heard a storm approaching, they would recite a verse—*Pierre, pierre, garde moi de la tonnerre* (Stone, stone, protect me from the thunder).

Many people in medieval Europe believed that ringing church bells would keep lightning away. In fact, church bells were often inscribed with the Latin words *Fulgura frango*, meaning "I break up the lightning strokes." During thunderstorms, bell ringers would run to their churches and ring the bells in an attempt to divert the lightning. This was extremely dangerous. In one 33-year period, 386 steeples received direct hits and 103 bell ringers were killed.

Finally, this superstition was proven false on April 15, 1718. On that day, twenty-four churches in Brittany, France, began ringing bells to ward off lightning. All twenty-four were struck while six churches, in which the bells were not ringing, were spared.

In medieval Europe, bell ringers would run to their churches and ring the bells to divert lightning—an extremely dangerous activity, as seen by the damage done by lightning to this modern church in Georgia.

Scientific Study

People didn't begin to seriously study lightning until the 1700s. In 1752, Benjamin Franklin—one of the founders of the United States—decided to conduct an experiment. He tied a metal key to the end of a kite string. Then he flew the kite in a thunderstorm. The potential (or voltage) that existed in the clouds during the electrical storm was carried by the wet string to the key. In this way, Franklin proved that lightning is electricity. *Franklin could have been killed while conducting this experiment. In fact, the next two people who tried this experiment were killed! You should never fly a kite in a thunderstorm.*

A year later, Franklin published a description of his new invention, the lightning rod. He built lightning rods for his own house and his friends' houses. In 1760, lightning struck the house of a Philadelphia merchant and the "Franklin rod" kept the property safe. Since the 1700s, we've learned a lot more about what causes lightning and how to protect ourselves and our property.

In 1752, Benjamin Franklin flew a kite with
a key tied to the string during a thunderstorm.
Because the kite's string was wet, the
voltage in the storm was carried to the key,
proving that lightning is electricity.

WHAT CAUSES LIGHTNING

CHAPTER 1

To understand lightning, you must first understand *atoms*. Everything in the universe is made of atoms, which are very tiny.

As small as atoms are, they're made of even smaller bits of matter called *protons*, *neutrons*, and *electrons*. The center, or *nucleus*, of the atom is made of protons and neutrons. Protons have a positive charge and neutrons have no charge at all. Electrons, which have a negative charge, whiz around the nucleus.

Most atoms have one proton for every electron, which means that the atom is balanced. It has no charge. However, an atom may gain or lose electrons during a chemical reaction or a collision with another atom. With this gain or loss, it becomes an *ion*. An ion with more electrons than protons has a negative charge; an ion with more protons than electrons has a positive charge.

These charges are important because opposite charges attract each other. A positive ion attracts a negative ion, but repels another positive ion.

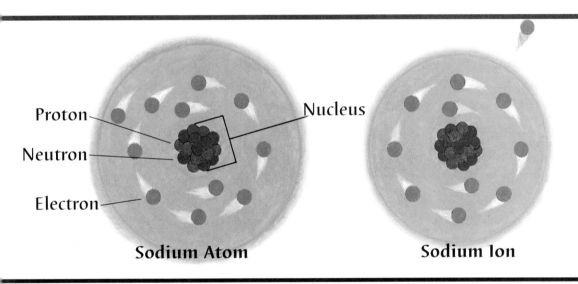

Proton
Nucleus
Neutron
Electron

Sodium Atom

Sodium Ion

An atom, such as this sodium atom, is made of positively-charged protons, negatively-charged electrons, and neutrons, which have no charge. Most atoms have no overall charge because they have one proton for every electron. When a sodium atom loses an electron, it becomes a sodium ion. A sodium ion has a positive charge.

Protons carry very strong positive charges, so electrons always flow toward protons. A lightning bolt is a signal that electrons are moving toward protons. To understand how this signal is created, we have to look at how a thundercloud forms.

How a Thundercloud Forms

Have you ever been to the beach on a hot sunny day? Think about how hot the sand was. You may have even seen waves of heat rising over the sand or over a hot paved road. As the ground heats up, the air above it heats up, too. When air heats up, the molecules that make up the air begin to move faster. As the molecules speed up, they move farther apart and take up more space. This makes the air expand—get bigger—and rise.

Some areas on the ground heat up more quickly than others. For example, a paved parking lot heats up more quickly than an area that is covered with grass. Similarly, the air above some areas heats up more quickly than the air above other areas. Only the air that heats up will expand and rise. The result is a tall column of hot, rising air. This column may be several miles high.

As the hot air rises higher and higher, it comes into contact with much cooler air and releases some of its heat. Because cool air can't hold as much mois-

How a Thunderstorm Forms

(5) Large water drops and ice crystals form at the top of the cloud and fall to earth.

(4) Water vapor condenses when it comes into contact with cooler air and clouds form.

(1) Light and heat from the sun strike Earth.

(3) Hot air expands and rises.

(2) The ground heats up.

ture as hot air, the water vapor in the column of air begins to condense and form tiny drops of water. Those condensed droplets of water, which are still too small to fall as rain, are what make up the clouds we see.

The condensing water releases heat and creates a strong updraft that pulls even more air from below. The cloud grows very rapidly at this point. In a few minutes, it can expand to more than 40,000 feet (12,000 m) tall and several miles wide.

At the top of the cloud, some of the water droplets collect to form larger drops. Eventually, the drops become heavy enough to fall to the ground. At about the same time, some of the water vapor starts to freeze into ice crystals, and they fall, too.

As the water drops and ice crystals fall through the cloud, they cool the cloud off. The hot air is still rising from the ground, but now it's not going straight up; instead, the cloud's cooler air is pushing the currents of warm air around. As all these currents of air swirl around each other, a strong wind forms in the thundercloud. The strong wind pulls some of the water drops apart. Scientists are not sure yet exactly how the positive and negative charges become separated, but they do know that the highest parts of the thundercloud become positively charged, while the lower parts become negatively charged.

The positive particles rise to the top of the cloud, while the negative particles settle to the bottom. As you learned earlier, positive charges attract negative charges. As the negative particles leap toward the positive particles, the movement of electrons creates a giant electrical spark, which we see as lightning. Thus, lightning is a signal to us that electrons are moving toward a location that has a greater concentration of positive charges.

At the beginning of a thunderstorm, the negative charges at the bottom of a cloud are usually attracted to the positive charges at the top of the same cloud. Lightning within a single cloud—called *intracloud lightning*—is the most common type of lightning.

The negative charges at the bottom of a cloud can also flow to the top of a different cloud. This is called *cloud-to-cloud lightning*. Lightning can flash between clouds that are 20 miles (32 km) apart. And sometimes the negative charges are attracted to positive charges in the surrounding air, creating *cloud-to-air lightning*.

The Making of a Lightning Bolt

At the beginning of a thunderstorm, most of the lightning flows within or between clouds. Eventually, however, so many negative particles build up at the bottoms of clouds that they begin leaking out into

23

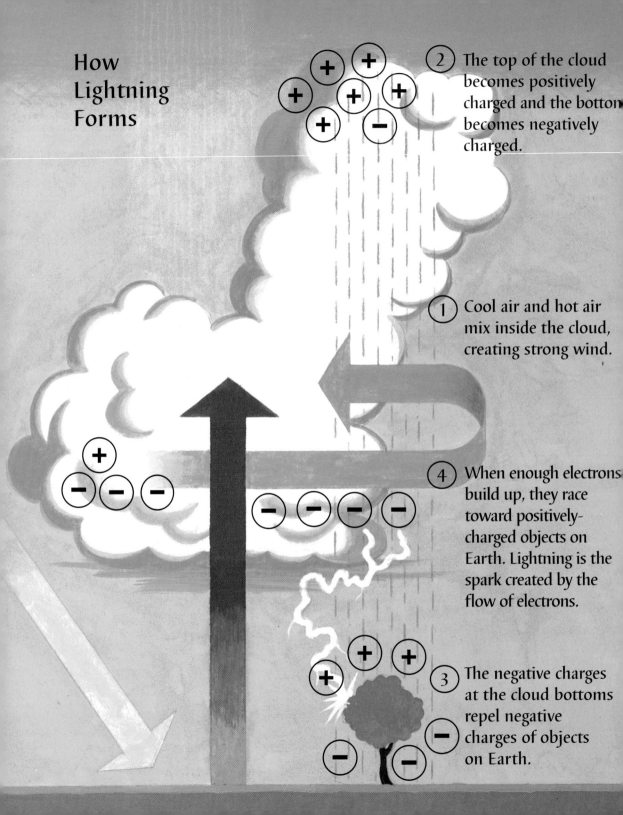

How Lightning Forms

2 The top of the cloud becomes positively charged and the bottom becomes negatively charged.

1 Cool air and hot air mix inside the cloud, creating strong wind.

4 When enough electrons build up, they race toward positively-charged objects on Earth. Lightning is the spark created by the flow of electrons.

3 The negative charges at the cloud bottoms repel negative charges of objects on Earth.

the air. The molecules in the air around the cloud pick up these electrons and they become negatively charged, too.

In the meantime, the negative charges at the bottom of the thundercloud repel electrons from the objects and ground under the cloud. As a result, the ground beneath the cloud becomes positively charged. When enough electrons build up around the cloud, they will be attracted to positively charged objects on earth. A flash of lightning is usually only a few inches wide, but it can be many miles long.

The first stroke of electrons to reach the ground is called the *stepped leader*. It moves downward in a series of steps. Each step is about 50 yards (45 m) long and lasts for only one-millionth of a second.

As the stepped leader gets close to the ground, positively charged leaders—often from tall objects like trees and buildings—travel up from the ground. Usually, the upward-moving leader from the tallest object is the first to meet the downward leader and complete the path between the ground and the cloud. That's why lightning usually hits the tallest object in an area.

Once the leader has made a path for the charge to move along, the lightning strokes back and forth from cloud to ground and back again. During each flash, the strokes usually go back and forth three to

four times, but they can travel back and forth more than twenty times.

The return stroke, from the ground to the cloud, creates the flash that people see. However, it happens so quickly that you can't tell that it's traveling upward. When you see lightning that seems to flicker, you're actually watching the individual strokes that make up a lightning flash. This type of lightning is called *cloud-to-ground lightning* or *ground-to-cloud lightning*, depending on the direction of the first charges.

Lightning strikes the top of the Eiffel Tower in Paris. The first stroke of electrons to reach the ground is called the stepped leader. It's met by a leader of positively charged electrons traveling up from the ground. The upward-moving leader from the tallest object is usually the first to meet the downward leader and complete the path between the ground and the cloud. This why lightning usually hits the tallest object in the area.

TYPES OF LIGHTNING

CHAPTER 2

When you think of lightning, you probably think of a bolt zigzagging down from the sky. Not all lightning looks like this, however. Even though all lightning is created in the same way, it can look very different depending on your location, the location of the discharge, and weather conditions.

Forked lightning, which is also called *streak lightning*, seems to zigzag down the sky. Streak lightning looks like a single jagged line of light. When lightning breaks up into a dotted line as it fades, it looks like a chain of beads in the sky. This is called *bead lightning* or *chain lightning*. *Ribbon lightning* looks like several streaks of lightning that flash to the ground together.

Forked or streak lightning appears to zigzag down the sky in a single jagged line of light.

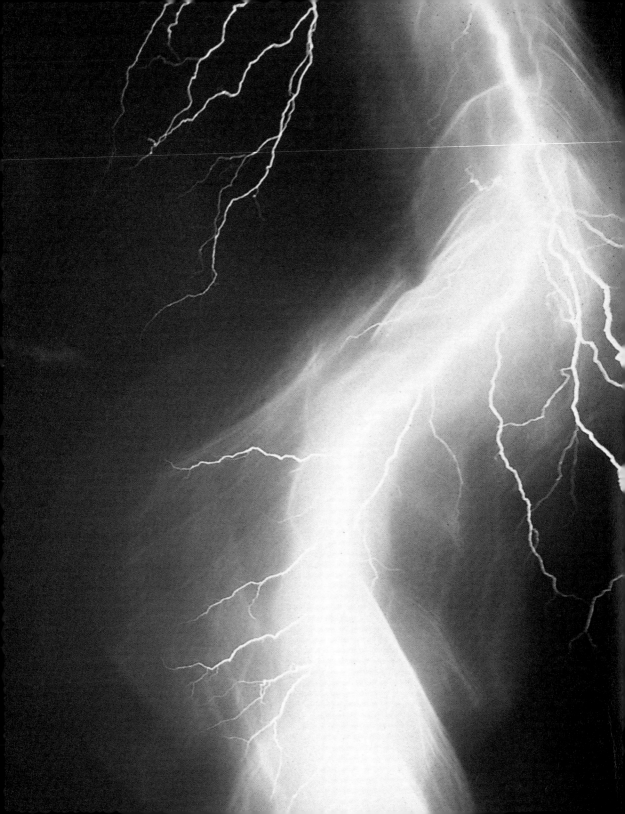

Sheet lightning seems to light up the sky in one bright flash. It is actually forked lightning, but it is so far away that you can't see the stroke. All you see is the flash reflected from clouds or scattered by droplets of water, dust, or smoke in the air. When lightning occurs so far away that you can't hear the thunder associated with it, it is called *heat lightning.*

Many sailors, airplane pilots, and mountain climbers have reported seeing a spooky but harmless glow called *St. Elmo's fire.* St. Elmo, the patron saint of sailors, was a fourth-century Italian bishop whose real name was probably Erasmus. When misty air ionizes around the tip of an object, such as a sailing ship's mast or an airplane's wing, electrons from the surrounding air are pulled toward the positive charge. This makes the air glow green. Unlike lightning, this ghostly fire doesn't damage the objects it touches.

According to legend, St. Elmo's fire is responsible for Ferdinand Magellan's successful voyage around the world in 1519. His crew was tired of stormy

This rare photo of ribbon lightning looks like several streaks of lightning that flashed to the ground together.

weather and ready to mutiny when they saw St. Elmo's fire on their ships' masts and spars. Because they believed that this phenomenon was a sign from

In this colored woodcut, people react to ball lightning. Witnesses say this rare type of light-ning looks like a glowing ball that floats for a few seconds or minutes and then vanishes or explodes.

heaven that the ocean would calm down, they decided to keep sailing.

For centuries, people have been reporting another unusual form of lightning, called *ball lightning*. Scientists don't know what causes ball lightning. In fact, a few say that it doesn't exist. These scientists believe that people who claim to see it have been taken in by an optical illusion—or have an overactive imagination.

Witnesses say that ball lightning looks like a glowing, fiery ball that floats for a few seconds or minutes and then vanishes or explodes. Most people claim that this ball of light is orange, red-orange, or white; some people have reported seeing blue, green, or yellow ball lightning. In some cases, the ball is as small as a marble. In other cases, it is as large as a basketball.

Some witnesses have reported that ball lightning floats along the ground or inside houses, barns, and airplanes. The glowing sphere sometimes floats into a building, through an open door or window, or comes down a chimney. Ball lightning can burn out lightbulbs, damage electrical wires, or scorch property.

On October 3, 1936, the London *Daily Mail* reported an amazing occurrence of ball lightning. Witnesses saw ball lightning cut through telephone wires, enter an open window, and dive into a barrel of water—causing the water to boil!

Volcanic lightning is created when a volcano erupts. The friction among the swirling particles of erupting ash creates static electricity, just as you do when you shuffle your feet as you walk across a carpet. When enough opposite charges build up, lightning flashes from one ash cloud to another or from a cloud to the earth. Such lightning was observed in the 1980 eruptions of Mount St. Helen's, a volcano in Washington's Cascade Mountains.

The *Pioneer Venus* spacecraft has detected low-frequency radio bursts coming from mountaintops on Venus. Some scientists think these radio bursts may be caused by lightning strokes. This evidence suggests that Venus, like Earth, may have volcanoes and volcanic lightning. (Lightning also generates radio signals here on Earth. In fact, when an AM radio is set to the upper end of the frequency dial, you can sometimes hear the sharp crackle of lightning strokes amid the static when a thunderstorm is approaching.)

Studying Lightning

What do scientists do when they want to study lightning? They make it come to them. The first lightning observatory was built in 1935 in Pittsfield,

When a volcano erupts, friction between the swirling
particles of erupting ash creates static electricity.
When enough opposite charges build up, volcanic
lightning occurs.

Pilots usually fly around thunderstorms to avoid lightning. Still, most commercial jets are struck by lightning about once a year.

Massachusetts. Researchers created a metal lab on top of the General Electric plant. The lab contained a periscope and camera to record lightning strikes.

Today, staff members at the Electric Power Research Institute use a 105-foot (32-m) "impulse generator" to make their own lightning. The generator can produce as many as 5.6 million volts of electricity—the voltage in just one bolt of lightning.

Scientists in New Mexico have called lightning down from the clouds by launching a 3-foot-tall (1-m-tall) rocket into a passing thundercloud. A spool of copper wire unwinds from the rocket's tail to create a path for the cloud's electrical charge. This path triggers a lightning strike. *Of course, you should never try to trigger lightning on your own!*

Thanks to the National Lightning Detection Network, scientists can now track lightning strikes all over the United States. The network is made up of hundreds of lightning sensors that, with the help of satellites, continually map lightning activity.

Other researchers test the lightning protection systems on airplanes to make sure the aircraft is safe. Although planes usually fly around thunderstorms to avoid lightning, most commercial jets are hit by lightning about once a year.

The planes usually aren't damaged, however, thanks to extensive research done on the ground.

Researchers zap models of new aircraft with a simulated lightning strike to find out where lightning is likely to enter and exit the plane. Protective devices on the plane's metal surface and framework provide a safe path for the electrical current to travel along. (You may notice these lightning *attenuators* the next time you're at the airport. They look like small molded metal strips along the plane's nose, tail, and fuselage.) Because lightning strikes produce strong electric and magnetic fields, planes also have special shields to protect their electronic guidance equipment.

Scientists are still finding new varieties of lightning. Recently, researchers recorded flashes of light that appear above thunderclouds. Some of these flashes look like red, carrot-shaped flashes, while others look like blue fountains of light.

Scientists have several theories to explain these strange lights. Some think that the tops of clouds become so highly charged that they create upside-down lightning superbolts. Others think the clouds create electric fields so large and strong that they make the air glow like a lightbulb. Despite extensive research, no one yet knows exactly what creates these stratospheric fireworks.

Other questions about lightning also remain unanswered. For example, scientists don't know how the negative cloud charge becomes large enough to trigger the first stroke of the lightning, why the number of lightning strikes is different in different months of the year, or how often lightning occurs over water. Although we've discovered a lot about lightning since the days of Ben Franklin, we still have a lot to learn!

THE EFFECTS OF LIGHTNING

CHAPTER 3

A lightning flash heats the air around it to 54,000 degrees Fahrenheit (30,000°C). This is five times hotter than the surface of the sun. This heat causes the air to expand at the speed of sound, creating a shock wave that we hear as thunder. If the storm is overhead, the thunder sounds like a huge bang. If the storm is farther away, the thunder can rumble for several seconds as the sound between the clouds and the ground or between hills.

A lightning bolt heats the air to 54,000 degrees Fahrenheit (30,000°C)—five times hotter than the sun's surface. This causes the air to expand at the speed of sound, creating the noise we hear as thunder.

40

You can tell how far away a storm is by measuring the amount of time between seeing the lightning flash and hearing thunder. For every 5 seconds between the two, the storm is 1 mile (1.6 km) away. To figure out how close a storm is, start counting when you see a flash of lightning by saying "one one-thousand, two one-thousand, three one-thousand" and so on. Stop counting when you hear the thunder. Divide the number by five, and you'll know how many miles away the storm is.

When lightning hits an object, the object is heated thousands of degrees in less than a second. Under such conditions, most objects vaporize or explode. Trees that have been hit by lightning often appear to have been blasted apart. That's because the moisture just under the bark is vaporized by the lightning and turned into heat, so the bark explodes.

When lightning strikes near electrical wires, a surge of current flows through them. These surges sometimes travel down power lines and into houses, where they can burn out appliances such as freezers, refrigerators, televisions, and computers. When lightning hits power lines, it also can blackout entire neighborhoods or cities.

When lightning hits sandy soil, the heat can fuse the sand along the path of the electricity, creating *fulgurites* (after the Latin word for lightning).

This fulgurite was created when lightning hit sandy soil. The lightning's heat fused the sand along its path.

These tubular structures may be more than 15 feet
(4.5 m) long.

The Benefits of Lightning

Some scientists think that lightning helped create life
on Earth. According to one theory, our planet's orig-
inal atmosphere contained methane, carbon dioxide,
hydrogen, ammonia, and water vapor. Lightning pro-
duced the energy that helped turn these substances
into organic molecules, which rained down into the
oceans. As time passed, these molecules became more
and more complex. Eventually, they developed into
the earliest forms of life.

The energy from lightning strokes also heats the
air enough to combine two gases, nitrogen and oxygen, into nitrous oxide. Rain dilutes this chemical
and delivers it to plants, which use it to grow. In
addition to serving as a natural fertilizer, this nitrogen becomes a part of the plant. When we eat the
plant, our bodies can absorb the nitrogen.

Although forest fires caused by lightning destroy
millions of acres of trees and brush each year, they
also serve a useful function. By burning thick under-
brush, they create space in the wilderness for cer-

*Lightning causes forest fires that destroy
millions of acres of trees and brush each year.*

tain plants and trees, such as the jack pine and the giant sequoia.

Lightning also changes some of the oxygen in the air into *ozone*, which helps clean the air. That's why everything smells clean and fresh after a storm. (You may have smelled ozone in any place where there is an electric spark, such as around electric toy trains.)

SAFETY TIPS

Your chances of being hit by lightning are quite small. About 1,500 people are struck by lightning each year in the United States. Of those, only 150 to 300 are killed, so the chances of being hit and killed are about 1 in 10. (The odds go up in central Florida, which has more lightning than any other part of the United States. The Pacific Northwest has almost no lightning.)

Some of the people who have survived being struck by lightning say they heard a brief, high-pitched whine and smelled sulfur or something burning. However, many others remember nothing at all. When they wake up, they're dazed and often find that they were thrown several feet from where they had been standing. They also sometimes discover

Although about 1,500 people are struck by lightning in the United States each year, only 150 to 300 are killed. Your chances of being struck by lightning are quite small.

that they're naked! That's because the lightning's electrical current vaporizes the moisture on human skin, which can literally blow a person's clothes off! Deaths caused by lightning are usually not due to burns. In most such cases, the lightning stops the victim's heart or lungs.

As you can see, lightning is very dangerous. These basic safety rules will help you avoid being hurt.

If You Are Outside

- If at all possible, you should go inside a building when a thunderstorm approaches.
- Sit inside a car. You'll be safe inside a car or truck because the rubber tires ground the vehicle. That means that if lightning does strike your car, it will travel through the metal and into the ground without hurting you. However, you must not touch any metal inside the car. Move away from open metal vehicles, such as bikes, golf carts, farm equipment, and motorcycles.

  Don't go inside a tent. A tent pole can actually attract lightning. Outdoor shelters without a lightning rod don't offer much protection. If the shelter is the highest spot in the landscape, it may be a target for lightning.
- Don't stand under a tree or on high ground. Since lightning is attracted to the highest object in the

area, do whatever you can to make sure that the highest object is not you! For example, do not stand on an empty beach or in an open field. If you're caught in the woods during a storm, take shelter under low shrubs or a group of trees that are all about the same height.

- Don't carry an umbrella. The metal rod could attract lightning.
- If you're in a swimming pool, lake, or the ocean as a thunderstorm approaches, get out of the water as quickly as possible, and move as far away from the water as you can.
- Stay away from overhead wires and metal fences. Also avoid metal poles (such as those that hold up clotheslines) and rails.
- If you feel your hair stand on end, you may be about to be struck by lightning. *Don't lie flat on the ground.* Instead, crouch down to make yourself as small as possible and balance on the balls of your feet to minimize your contact with the ground. (That lowers your chances of being hit by electric current spreading through the ground.)

Lightning is attracted to the highest object in an area, so you should never stand under a tree or on high ground during a thunderstorm.

If You Are Indoors

- Don't touch electrical appliances or plumbing fixtures. Use the phone only in an emergency.
- Stay away from open doors, windows, and fireplaces. (It is safe to watch a lightning storm from behind a closed window.)
- Stay out of the bathtub or shower.

Myths About Lightning

- Lightning poses no danger if it's not raining. False. Lightning can strike tens of miles away from any rainfall.
- You shouldn't touch people who have been struck by lightning because the electrical charge may transfer from them to you. False. Victims of lightning don't carry any electrical charge. If you or someone you know gets struck by lightning, you should seek medical attention as soon as possible. Cardiopulmonary resuscitation (CPR) can often save a victim of lightning.
- Lightning never strikes the same place twice. False. Lightning usually strikes the highest object, so tall buildings, such as the Empire State Building in New York City, may be struck thousands of times.

GETTING CLOSER TO LIGHTNING

CHAPTER 5

If you have a camera with a manual focus and a tripod, you can take your own photographs of lightning. You do not even need to go outside. You will be much safer if you stay inside and take photos through a closed window.

Begin by finding a window that offers an unobstructed view of the sky. Set up a tripod to steady your camera. If possible, use a cable release to help keep the camera from moving. Use a slow slide film for high resolution. The best film speed is ASA 100, which lets you use the maximum exposure time.

Start shooting with your *f-stop* set at about 11 at night or about 22 during the day. Experiment with

The safest way to photograph lightning is to stay inside and shoot through a closed window. You'll need a camera with a manual focus and a tripod.

different exposures and lenses to see what gives you the best results.

Don't use autofocus. If you do, the camera may focus on a nearby branch or power line, rather than on the more distant lightning. Instead, set your camera's focus on manual and infinity. Be sure to frame your picture so that it includes some ground—perhaps even a tree or car—to give perspective.

When you take your film to be developed, ask the clerk to print only the negatives that actually show a lightning bolt. Otherwise, you'll have to pay for printing all the photos that didn't manage to capture any lightning at all.

If you'd like to check out lightning in a more controlled environment, visit one of the many science museums around the country that have exhibits on lightning, static electricity, and related phenomena. Check your local phone book or contact the following organization for a science museum or traveling exhibit in your area:

Association of Science-Technology Centers, Inc.
1025 Vermont Ave., Suite 500
Washington, DC 20005
(202) 783-7200 phone
(202) 783-7207 fax

GLOSSARY

atom—the basic unit of matter.

attenuator—a device that reduces the amplitude of an electrical signal.

ball lightning—a rare type of lightning that looks like a glowing, fiery ball and that floats for several seconds before vanishing.

bead lightning—lightning that breaks up into a dotted line as it fades so that it looks like a chain of beads in the sky (also called chain lightning).

chain lightning—see bead lightning.

cloud-to-air lightning—lightning that flashes from a cloud to the surrounding air.

cloud-to-cloud lightning—lightning that jumps from one cloud to another.

cloud-to-ground lightning—lightning that flashes from a cloud to the ground.

electron—a small bit of matter that carries a negative charge and which orbits the nucleus of an atom.

forked lightning—lightning that seems to zigzag down the sky.

f-stop—a measurement of a lens opening on a camera.

fulgurite—a formation formed when lightning hits sandy soil and fuses the sand into a rocklike substance along the electricity's path.

ground-to-cloud lightning—lightning that flashes from the ground to the cloud.

heat lightning—lightning that strikes so far away that the accompanying thunder can't be heard.

intracloud lightning—lightning that occurs inside a cloud.

ion—an atom that carries either a positive or negative charge because it has lost or gained an electron.

neutron—a small bit of matter that carries no electrical charge. Neutrons, along with protons, are found in the nucleus of an atom.

nucleus—a group of protons and neutrons that form the center of an atom.

ozone—a form of oxygen created when electricity passes through the air.

proton—a small bit of matter that carries a positive charge. Protons, along with neutrons, are found in the nucleus of an atom.

ribbon lightning—lightning that looks like several streaks of lightning flashing to the ground together.

St. Elmo's fire—a type of lightning that looks like a green glow and that appears around the tip of objects, such as sailboat masts or airplane wings.

sheet lightning—lightning that strikes so far away that the actual stroke can't be seen and that seems to light up the sky in one bright flash.

stepped leader—the first stroke of electrons from a cloud to the ground, which creates a path for the lightning to follow.

Stone Age—the period in history when humans began using stone tools.

streak lightning—lightning that looks like a single jagged line of light.

volcanic lightning—lightning that is created when a volcano erupts.

ADDITIONAL INFORMATION

Books

Cosgrove, Brian. *Weather*. New York: Alfred A. Knopf, 1991.

Simon, Seymour. *Storms*. New York: William Morrow and Company, 1989.

Trefil, James. *Meditations at Sunset: A Scientist Looks at the Sky*. New York: Macmillan, 1987.

Wagner, Ronald L. and Bill Adler, Jr. *The Weather Sourcebook: Your One-Stop Resource for Everything You Need to Feed Your Weather Habit*. Old Saybrook, CT: Adler & Robin Books, Inc., 1994.

Watson, Benjamin A. and the editors of *The Old Farmer's Almanac. The Old Farmer's Almanac Book of*

Weather and Natural Disasters. New York: Random House, 1993.

Williams, Jack. *The Weather Book: An Easy-to-Understand Guide to the USA's Weather.* New York: Vintage, 1992.

Magazine Articles

Acerrano, Anthony. "Lightning: Don't Get Hit." *Sports Afield.* May 1994, pp. 98–100.

Bankson, Russ. "Why Does Lightning Happen?" *National Geographic World.* August 1992, pp. 22–23.

Horstmeyer, Steve. "Rolling Thunder." *Weatherwise.* December 1993, pp. 24–26.

Pearce, Q.L. "Nature's Fireworks." *Disney Adventures.* October 1991, pp. 78–79.

Zimmer, Carl. "Carrots Over Nebraska." *Discover.* January 1995, pp. 67–68.

"Against All Odds: U.S. Serviceman Struck by Lightning." *USA.* August 1995, pp. 21–23.

"Don't Get Shocked." *Safety and Health.* April 1994, p. 89.

Internet Resources

Due to the changeable nature of the Internet, sites appear and disappear very quickly. These resources offer useful information on lightning at the time of publication.

The National Lightning Safety Institute's site offers photos and text on the effects of lightning and lightning safety. Its address is **http://www.lightning safety.com/**.

The *USA Today* Weather Page has basic information about weather, including lightning, and can be reached at **http://www.usatoday.com/weather/wtsm0.htm**.

The Lightning Page has lightning photos, maps of lightning strikes that occurred in the last week, and answers to frequently asked questions about lightning. It can be reached at **http://www.wvit-coe.wvnet.edu/drobinso/**.

You can also see a United States map that shows last week's lightning strikes at **http://alden.com/light1.html**.

The Storm Prediction Center monitors and forecasts storms. Its site is at **http://www.awc.kc.noaa.gov/spc/**.

INDEX

Page numbers in *italics* indicate photographs and illustrations.

ABOUT THE
AUTHOR

Suzanne Harper is the executive editor of *Disney Adventures* and has published numerous magazine and newspaper articles. She earned journalism and English degrees from the University of Texas-Austin and a master's degree in writing from the University of Southern California. She lives in New York City.